KEEPING CUSTOMERS
FOR LIFE

Better Management Skills

This highly popular range of inexpensive paperbacks covers all areas of basic management. Practical, easy to read and instantly accessible, these guides will help managers to improve their business or communication skills. Those marked * are available on audio cassette.

The books in this series can be tailored to specific company requirements. For further details, please contact the publisher, Kogan Page, telephone 0171 278 0433, fax 0171 837 6348.

Be a Successful Supervisor
Business Etiquette
Coaching Your Employees
Creative Decision-making
Creative Thinking in Business
Delegating for Results
Effective Employee Participation
Effective Meeting Skills
Effective Performance Appraisals*
Effective Presentation Skills
Empowerment
First Time Supervisor
Get Organised!
Goals and Goal Setting
How to Communicate Effectively*
How to Develop a Positive Attitude*
How to Develop Assertiveness
How to Motivate People*
How to Understand Financial Statements
How to Write a Staff Manual
Improving Employee Performance
Improving Relations at Work
Leadership Skills for Women

Learning to Lead
Make Every Minute Count*
Managing Disagreement Constructively
Managing Organisational Change
Managing Part-Time Employees
Managing Quality Customer Service
Managing Your Boss
Marketing for Success
Memory Skills in Business
Mentoring
Office Management
Productive Planning
Project Management
Quality Customer Service
Rate Your Skills as a Manager
Sales Training Basics
Self-managing Teams
Selling Professionally
Successful Negotiation
Successful Telephone Techniques
Systematic Problem-solving
Team Building
Training Methods that Work

KEEPING CUSTOMERS FOR LIFE

Richard F Gerson

KOGAN
PAGE

This book is dedicated to my wife Robbie and our sons Michael and Mitchell, who continue to teach me the true meaning of satisfaction in life. Thank you all.

Copyright © Crisp Publications Inc 1992

All rights reserved. No part of this book may be reproduced or transmitted in any form or by any means now known or to be invented, electronic or mechanical, including photocopying, recording, or by any information storage or retrieval system, without written permission from the author or publisher, except for the brief inclusion of quotations in a review.

First published in the United States of America in 1992 by Crisp Publications Inc, 1200 Hamilton Court, Menlo Park, California 94025, USA, entitled *Beyond Customer Service*.

This edition first published in Great Britain in 1993 by Kogan Page Ltd, 120 Pentonville Road, London N1 9JN, reprinted 1995.

British Library Cataloguing in Publication Data

A CIP record for this book is available from the British Library.

ISBN 0-7494-0944-4

Typeset by BookEns Ltd, Royston, Herts.
Printed and bound in Great Britain by Clays Ltd, St. Ives plc.

Contents

About This Book   7

1. Customer Service and Beyond   9
Developing superior customer service programmes 9
Seven steps to a successful customer service system 14
Keeping your customers 17
Reasons for poor service 20

2. Customer Retention   23
Developing customer retention programmes 23
Retention through value chains 26
Retention through customer service marketing 31
Retention through recovery 43
Retention through training 48
Retention through rapport and effective
   communication 51

3. 50 Ways to Keep Your Customers for Life   59

Appendix 1. Customer Service Tips and Lists   71
Appendix 2. Customer Service, Satisfaction and
   Retention Surveys   77
Appendix 3. Customer Information and Profile   83

Further Reading from Kogan Page   87

About This Book

Keeping Customers for Life is a very useful resource for both small and large business owners – in fact, for everyone who wants to compete in today's marketplace. With so many businesses offering similar products and services, one of the only ways left to compete is to exceed traditional customer service. This book will tell you how to extend your customer service programme into a customer retention programme.

Each chapter is a stand-alone unit that explains how to retain your customers for life. Read each chapter all the way through, then go back to the particular sections that will help you to develop your customer retention programme. Remember to use the retention and service techniques as marketing tools to maintain your competitive edge.

Do not rush through this book. Read everything carefully. Take notes. Think about your customer service programme, its policies and procedures, and how you can improve the entire system. Customer service is necessary for success in today's business environment. So is customer satisfaction. However, continued success is based on long-term customer retention. This book will provide you with the methods and tactics to keep your customers for life.

CHAPTER 1
Customer Service and Beyond

Developing superior customer service programmes

In today's volatile economy, providing excellent customer service can be the critical difference in your company's success.

Customer service does not only mean producing high quality products, although product quality is an important part of customer service. People don't tolerate shoddy goods – they return them and shop somewhere else. First, you must sell customers quality products to win them over. Then you must provide superior customer service to keep them.

Customer service involves all the activities which your business and your employees conduct or perform to satisfy customers. This means more than just handling complaints, providing refunds or exchanges on returns, and smiling at customers. Customer service also means going out of your way for the customer, doing everything possible to satisfy the customer, and making decisions that benefit the customer even at the expense of your company.

The importance of customer service
Recall how you felt the last time you had poor service, either at a restaurant, an airport ticket desk or a retail store. In the space provided, describe the situation, what was said, how you felt, what was done and your expectations about purchasing from that provider again. If you decided never to shop there again, what do you think it cost that company not to satisfy you and keep you as a customer?

The cost of poor customer service

Customer service pays, it does not cost. It pays in many ways, the first of which is long-term customer retention. Many businesses understand the cost of acquiring a customer, but they don't understand the cost of losing one. In fact, it costs five to six times more to acquire a customer than it does to do business with a current or former customer.

Work out how much it costs to lose a customer. The formula is based on information from the US Office of Consumer Affairs. You need to know three figures to complete the formula: your annual sales revenue, the number of customers you have and the cost of acquiring and keeping them, including marketing, sales, advertising, promotions, discounts, etc. You can use cash amounts or the percentage of sales to help you determine the cost of poor service.

What you lose

Let us assume that your hypothetical business has a sales revenue of £10 million a year from 2500 customers. We will also assume that the cost of sales if 66 per cent of revenue, or £6.6 million. Now, put these figures into the formula on page 11 and see what poor customer service really costs your company.

Take the total number of customers and multiply it by 25 per cent to get the number of dissatisfied customers. Then multiply that result by 70 per cent, which is an estimate of the number of dissatisfied customers who will stop doing business with you. Divide the total annual sales revenue by the number of customers to get the average revenue of one customer, then multiply this by the number who switched, and you get the cost of losing your customers.

Next, calculate your lost opportunity revenue by assuming each dissatisfied customer will tell 10 people. Assume that 2 per cent of them will buy elsewhere. Multiply this number by the average revenue per customer and you get your potential lost revenue.

To determine your customer acquisition and replacement costs, multiply your total annual sales revenue by 66 per cent, and divide that by your total number of customers to get your average cost per customer. Multiply this result by 5 to get your replacement cost per customer.

Now, add up all your results to get the total cost of poor service. Multiply that figure by 10 to determine the costs of poor service over a 10-year period, considered to be the customer's lifetime for doing business with you.

No business of any size can afford to lose and seek customers continuously. These results should motivate you to improve your customer service programmes so that they become customer retention programmes.

The cost of poor service

Lost customer revenue

A.	Annual sales revenue	£	10,000,000
B.	Total number of customers		2,500
C.	Percentage of dissatisfied customers	×	.25
D.	Number of dissatisfied customers (C × B)	=	625
E.	Percentage of dissatisfied customers who are likely to switch	×	.70
F.	Number of dissatisfied customers who will switch	=	437.5
G.	Average revenue per customer (A ÷ B)	£	4,000
H.	Revenue lost through poor service (F × G)	£	(1,750,000)

Lost opportunity revenue

I.	Number of other people whom dissatisfied customers tell (F × 10)		4,375
J.	Number of potential customers who buy elsewhere owing to negative work of mouth (assume one in 50 tell, therefore 1 × .02)		87.5
K.	Potential lost revenue (J × G)	£	(350,000)

Customer replacement costs
L. Customer acquisition costs (66% × A)   £   6,600,000
M. Average cost per customer (L ÷ B)   2,640
N. Replacement cost for lost customers
    (M × 5)   £   (13,200)

Total costs
O. Total annual cost (H + K + N)   £   (2,113,200)
P. Total cost over customer's lifetime of doing
    business for 10 years (O × 10)   £ (21,132,000)

As you can see from this frightening example, our hypothetical company will lose more than £2 million a year owing to poor service and customer retention. Now fill in the same chart for your company. Your results will probably motivate you to improve your customer service and retention efforts.

The cost of poor service

Fill in this chart for your own company.

Lost customer revenue
A. Annual sales revenue   £_____
B. Total number of customers   _____
C. Percentage of dissatisfied customers   ×   .25
D. Number of dissatisfied customers (C × B)   =_____
E. Percentage of dissatisfied customers who are
    likely to switch   ×   .70
F. Number of dissatisfied customers who will
    switch   =_____
G. Average revenue per customer (A ÷ B)   £_____
H. Revenue lost through poor service (F × G)   £_____

Lost opportunity revenue

I. Number of other people whom dissatisfied
    customers tell (F × 10) _____

J. Number of potential customers who buy else-
    where owing to negative word of mouth
    (assume one in 50 tell, therefore 1 × .02) _____

K. Potential lost revenue (J × G) £_____

Customer replacement costs

L. Customer acquisition costs (____% × A) £_____

M. Average cost per customer (L ÷ B) £_____

N. Replacement cost for lost customers (M × 5) £_____

Total costs

O. Total annual cost (H + K + N) £_____

P. Total cost over customer's lifetime of doing
    business for 10 years (O × 10) £_____

Customer service: One, two three

Poor customer service is expensive. Good customer service is invaluable, and you can achieve it in your company. First, you must realise that service is both a marketing and a management tool for your business. It enhances marketing because it motivates customers to spread the good word about your service and business to others. Remember, the least expensive way to acquire new customers is through word of mouth.* Good service makes management easier because everybody is committed to satisfying the customer. The results will be increased productivity and profits simply because management and employees are working to achieve the same goal.

Next, develop a customer service system for your company that is easy for your customers to use.†

Last, design and implement customer retention programmes that will maintain customer loyalty, thereby increasing the

---

*See Harris, Godfrey and Harris, Gregrey, *Talk is Cheap* (Kogan Page).

†See Martin, William B, *Managing Quality Customer Service* (Kogan Page).

probability that your customers will refer new buyers to your business. Also, remember to use these retention programmes as both primary and supplementary marketing tools.

Seven steps to a successful customer service system

Developing a successful customer service system can be one of the most rewarding goals you achieve for your company. Like most goals, it requires planning and work. Following these seven steps will place you ahead of your competition and start you on your way to successful customer retention.

1. Total management commitment
Customer service programmes cannot succeed within a company unless top management is committed to the concept. It is up to the managing director, chief executive or owner to develop a clear and concise service vision for the company. Then management must communicate that vision, as the company's service mission statement, to all the employees. Use the space below to write your own vision or mission statement for customer service and retention.

_____

_____

_____

_____

2. Get to know your customers
Not only must you get to know your customers intimately, you must also understand them totally. You need to know what they like about you, what they dislike, what they want changed, how they want it changed, what needs they have, what their expectations are, what motivates them to buy, what satisfies them and what you must continue to do to maintain their loyalty. The most effective way to get this information is simply to ask your customers.*

_____

*See Curry, Jay, _Know your Customers!_ (Kogan Page).

Once you start to know your customers, you must continue to learn about them. Their needs change on a regular – even daily – basis and you must keep up with them. Make it a policy to phone your customers at least once a month to find out how they are doing and what they need. While this shows them that you are interested in providing good customer service, it also helps you to develop effective customer retention programmes because it tells your customers that you are interested in them as people.

3. Develop standards of quality service performance
Customer service is not as intangible a concept as you may think. Each business has specific business practices that could be improved. For example, how many times does the phone ring before someone answers it? How many call transfers does it take to find someone to answer the customer's question? How long does it take to process an order or ship a replacement? When standards are set for ordinary business practices, you can be assured of superior performance by your employees. Remember, what gets measured gets done.

4. Recruit, train and reward good staff
Good customer service and effective customer retention programmes can be provided only by competent, qualified people. Your service is only as professional as the people who deliver it. If you want your business to be good to people, recruit good people.

Then train them to provide the ultimate in customer service and retention. Be sure that they understand what your company's standards of service are. Reward them well because they are the primary contact that your customers have with your company and the reason why people will continue to do business with you. Also, these people *are* your company in the eyes and minds of the customers.

Give your staff the authority to make decisions on the spot to satisfy customers. Remember that serving and retaining customers is one of the hardest jobs in a company. If people have that responsibility, they must also have the authority to decide what they can do for a customer.

5. Reward service accomplishments

Always recognise, reward and reinforce superior performance. Provide financial and psychological rewards and incentives for your staff. Recognise the small gains and accomplishments in the same way as you would applaud the major gains.

You must also reward your customers for good customer behaviour. They appreciate recognition in the same way as your employees. Recognising your customers will go a long way towards retaining them and having them refer new people to you.

6. Stay close to your customers

Always stay in touch with your customers. Conduct continuous research in order to learn from them. Ask them questions after they make a purchase, send them surveys in the post, run contests that require participation in a survey, phone them up, develop a customer council to advise you on their needs, and do anything else you can to stay close to your customers. Most important of all, *listen* to them.

Your relationship with the customer actually begins after the purchase is made. This is when you must activate your retention programmes, and this is when the customer will see how much you really care. Arrange all customer interactions so they are win–win situations for both of you. The result will be more loyal customers.

7. Work towards continuous improvement

Even though you have designed friendly and accessible customer service systems, recruited and trained the best people and gone out of your way to learn about and satisfy your customers' needs, you must remember that no system, business or programme is perfect. Therefore, you must continuously work to improve your customer service and retention programmes.

Your attempts at continuous improvement will be viewed positively by the customers and your employees. They will see that you are trying to become even better than you already are. And when you become better, your service to them will also be better. The result is more satisfied customers, more business for you and your staff, and greater profits.

Customer service pays, it does not cost. You must constantly work to provide the best service at all times. Your only goal for being in business should be to satisfy your customers. Once this is done, the growth, expansion and profits will take care of themselves. Follow these seven steps to implementing a customer service system, and you will find that it will be easy for you to go beyond customer service.

Keeping your customers

Customers today are better educated than ever before. They are more careful about their purchases and the money they spend. They want value for money. They also want good service and they are willing to pay for it. But who are these customers, and how do you know when they're happy?

Startling service statistics

- Only 4 per cent of customers ever complain. This means that your business may never hear from 96 per cent of its customers, and 91 per cent of those just go away because they feel that complaining will not do them any good. In fact, complainers are more likely to continue doing business with you than non-complainers.
- For every complaint your business receives, there are 26 other customers with unresolved complaints or problems, and six of those customers have serious problems. These are people who you will probably never hear from. These are also people who can tell you how to make your business better. Get their feedback any way you can.
- Most customers who complain to you (54–70 per cent) will do business with you again if you resolve their complaint. If they feel that you acted quickly and to their satisfaction, up to 95 per cent of them will do business with you again, and they will probably refer other people to you.

- A dissatisfied customer will tell up to 10 people about it. Approximately 13 per cent of those will tell up to 20 people about their problem. You cannot afford the advertising to overcome this negative word of mouth.
- Happy customers, or customers who have had their complaints resolved, will tell between three and five people about their positive experience. Therefore, you have to satisfy three to four customers for every one who is dissatisfied with you. It is very difficult in any business to work with a 4:1 ratio against you. Customer retention programmes will enhance the value of your customer service efforts.
- It costs five to six times more to attract new customers than to keep old ones, even when you have to go back and renew contacts with former customers. Additionally, customer loyalty and the lifetime value of a customer can be worth up to 10 times as much as the price of a single purchase.
- Businesses that provide superior customer service can charge more, realise greater profits, increase their market share and have customers willingly pay more for their products simply because of the good service. In fact, you can gain an average of 6 per cent a year in market share simply by providing good service: satisfying and keeping your customers.
- The lifetime value of a customer, or the amount of purchases that customer would make over 10 years, is worth more than the cost of returning the purchase price of one item. For example, supermarkets realise up to £5000 a year from one family. That means £50,000 over 10 years. Is it worth it for them to provide refunds when the customer returns a purchase? Is it worth it to you to have the goodwill and positive word of mouth that this type of retention service will bring you?
- Customer service is governed by the rule of 10s. If it costs £10,000 to get a new customer, it takes only 10 seconds to lose one, and 10 years to get over it or for the problem to be resolved. You must work to keep your customers.
- Customers stop doing business with you because:

—1 per cent die
—3 per cent move away
—5 per cent seek alternatives or develop other business relationships
—9 per cent begin doing business with the competition
—14 per cent are dissatisfied with the product or service
—68 per cent are upset with the treatment they have received.

If you look at these percentages, you actually have some control over 96 per cent of the reasons why customers stop doing business with you.

What can you do?

Write down the reasons why you think people might stop doing business with you. Obviously, poor service is one of them, but what other reasons come to mind? After you write down a reason, describe what you would do to correct the problem.

Reasons to stop doing business	Solutions

These statistics, and the chart that helped you to calculate the cost of losing customers, emphasise the importance of customer retention programmes. It is no longer enough to say that your company provides good customer service. Nor is it enough to train and empower your people to offer the service behaviour that will satisfy the customers. It is only through customer retention programmes that you will be able to maintain your market share and competitive edge, keep your current customers and remain profitable.

Reasons for poor service

Ask any consumer why companies give poor service, and he or she will tell you. Some problems are common to many businesses. How many of them apply to your organisation? Does your company have any unique service problems?

- Uncaring employees
- Poor employee training
- Negative attitudes of employees towards customers
- Differences in perception between what businesses think customers want and what customers actually want
- Differences in perception between the product or service that businesses think they provide and what customers think they receive
- Differences in perception between the way businesses think customers want to be treated and the way customers really want to be treated, or are actually treated.
- No customer service philosophy within the company
- Poor handling and resolution of complaints
- Employees are not empowered to provide good service, take responsibility and make decisions that will satisfy the customer
- Poor treatment of employees as customers.

Remember that people are loyal to a business because they feel that they are treated well, they receive good value for their money and they are psychologically or physically attached to the business. You must do everything possible to make certain that your customers do not want to switch to your competitors.

Shoppers are price conscious. They will often switch brands or business suppliers simply because one provides a price advantage over the other. You can prevent this by providing superior customer service and employing customer retention strategies. Make it hard for them to leave you. Establish a personal relationship with your customers so that you maintain their loyalty and they continue to do business with you.

Never take a customer for granted. Be grateful that they have decided to do business with you and not a competitor. Work as hard as you possibly can to deliver more than they expect, and you will have gone a long way towards retaining your customers.

CHAPTER 2
Customer Retention

Developing customer retention programmes

Customer service does not exist in a vacuum and neither do customer retention programmes. You need an overall structure or guiding focus to make them work. Consider marketing as that guiding principle, and create all your customer retention programmes under your marketing umbrella. This will enable you to track and evaluate your efforts. Once you set up the programmes within the marketing plan, you can use customer service as an effective yet inexpensive marketing tool.

Most companies think of customer service as something they do after the fact. They view the process more as a complaint-handling system than a marketing technique. Complaint handling is only one small part of customer service. You must make the decision now to develop superior customer service and retention programmes that are proactive, rather than reactive.

Proactive v reactive efforts

Customer service has two sides. Reactive customer service comes after the fact – after a customer has had a problem, a complaint, is dissatisfied or has had to bring something to the attention of a business. Proactive service begins even before the customer walks in the door. Your business is already prepared to do everything possible to satisfy and keep the customer.

One of the best examples of proactive service is making the buying experience as easy as possible for the customer. Speed up the purchase process, decrease waiting times (people hate waiting), make your business a nice place to be. Many businesses, especially service businesses, do not have a tangible item to sell. Therefore, the office, the appearance of the facility or the staff, is the only tangible item that the customer sees. You must make it pleasant and appealing. People will continue to do business with you because they like the way you look and this makes them feel comfortable.

Proactive service and retention does wonders for a company's bottom line. Add to this some other retention-getters, such as thanking customers for coming in, thanking them for shopping even when they do not buy, and offering them additional information so that they can make a better purchase decision. You will find that they will keep coming back to you simply because you created a pleasant atmosphere, made it a nice place for them to shop and made it easy for them to buy.

Think of ways in which you can be proactive in the service you provide for customers. What can you do for them so that they will want to continue to do business with you? Write down your ideas, then try to implement one idea a week. You will be pleasantly surprised at the results.

Internal *and* external service

Everybody thinks of customer service as something you do to, or for, those people who buy from you. But another group of customers also deserves good service, and that group is your staff. Everyone who works for you or with you is also a customer. You must provide your employees with the same type of superior service and retention efforts as the buyers of your products. You cannot expect employees to provide excellent customer service if they are not treated well by their employer.

Ask yourself another question and write the answer below. Then check it with the explanation that follows.

Whom do you work for?

_____

Your simple, one-line answer should have been the customer. If you are an employer or a business owner, you work for the buying customer and your employee customer. If you are an employee, you work for the buying customer and the other people who depend upon your work. Basically, if you are not directly serving the buying customer, you are probably working for someone who is.

Employees as customers

Employees are customers too. So are their families and your shareholders. You must work to serve and retain them. You already know the cost of poor service to a buying customer. Now, what does poor service to an employee cost? You must include:

- Lost salaries paid to employees who have left the company
- Recruitment costs of new employees
- Training costs for new employees
- Turnover as a percentage of sales and profits
- Negative image as a company with high turnover.

Do you have any additional factors that may be included in the cost of not retaining your employees?

Employee retention is simply a function of superior internal customer service. Recruit and train the best people with the best people attitudes. Then empower them to make decisions. Give them authority to go with their responsibility of serving the customer. Recognise and reward their accomplishments and achievements. Treat them as you would your best customers. You will see tremendous results, such as lower recruiting and replacement costs, because more people will stay with you longer. These people will recommend people to work for you so you do not have to spend money on recruiting. Above all, remember that if you serve your employees well, they will serve you and your customers well.

Retention through value chains

A chain is only as strong as its weakest link. As a business, you have suppliers and final customers, with employees in between. This is your value chain. Set it up so that every link is strong.

Treat your suppliers well. Order what you know they can deliver. Expect delivery within a reasonable amount of time. Pay your bills on time. Reward their loyalty with more business. Create enhanced value for them so that they will continue to do business with you.

Treat your employees well. They deserve it and your customers deserve it.

Treat your customers well. Listen to them. Find out what they need, want and expect. Then give them everything and more. Exceed their expectations. Put more value in the chain. Let them know who your suppliers are and how well you treat your employees. This will make them comfortable and secure with you, and they will continue to do business with you.

Value chain
Draw your own value chain below. A basic three link chain has been provided for you. Follow it or create your own. Then list the actions that you can take to add more value to your customer interactions.

Actions

_____

_____

_____

_____

Value-added service
Drawing the value chain is the first step to providing value-added service. Value-added service means giving the customers more than they expect. Sometimes you can charge more for value-added service because customers will pay the added price just to receive the quality service.

An example of value-added service is the concept of the 'baker's dozen': you pay for 12 items and receive 13. Some companies have extended this idea to give you 14 or 15 items for the price of 12. This is their attempt to compete by providing value-added service.

Perhaps an employee decides that customer satisfaction is more important than company policy. For example, some companies have policies stating that refunds or exchanges will be made only with the original sales receipt and packaging within 30 days of purchase. If you have ever brought something back on the 31st day, or without the receipt, and had a company representative accept it from you, you received value-added service.

By doing this, the representative ensures that you will be a satisfied customer and that you will continue to do business with the company. On the other hand, if you brought the item back, were treated rudely and told that the policy forbids late exchanges, how would you feel? Would you do business with the company again? Probably not.

To see how well you're doing with your customers, check out the competition to see what they are doing with value-added service enhancements. If they are doing something that you like, adapt it and make it work for your company.

Use the chart below to help you.

Competitor's service policy	What I like	How I will adapt it

Now let's see how you can introduce value-added enhancements to your business.

Fill in the chart opposite to help you provide value-added service as a customer retention tool. Write your current customer service programmes in the left-hand column and the ways in which you will add value to them in the right-hand column. When you have completed the chart, describe how these new value-added service enhancements will help your business.

Company policies	Value-added enhancements
1.	
2.	
3.	
4.	
5.	
6.	
7.	
8.	
9.	
10.	

These enhancements will help my business by:

1. _____

2. _____

3. _____

4. _____

5. _____

Service enhancements

Value-added service can be expanded to include service enhancements, which are basically the services that you already offer with some improvements.

For example, let us assume that you are a car dealer who guarantees repair work for six months or the car is repaired again, free. A service enhancement to this policy would be to lend the owner a car while you work on his car. If it is the second or third time that you are trying to fix the same problem, and the fault is yours, you can refund the money for the original repair, just because your customer was inconvenienced by bringing the car back again.

Or you could give a free gift with a purchase. This creates the impression that people are getting more for their money. And you know how everyone likes a bargain.

What other types of service enhancements can you provide? Perhaps you can offer toll-free telephone numbers, free service calls or replacement parts for products under guarantee or warranty. List your service enhancements and why they would interest your customers. Be very specific when you list the benefits, as these become excellent marketing and advertising messages.

Current service	Service enhancement	Benefit

Retention through customer service marketing

Your business doesn't have to be on a seesaw of losing customers and seeking new ones. You can go beyond customer service, increase customer retention and enhance your marketing efforts all at the same time. In fact, your customer retention policies double as excellent marketing approaches for your business.

Do the following quiz. Answer each question with a 'Yes' or 'No'. On a separate sheet of paper, describe why you do or do not perform any of the following activities.

Does your business engage in:

	Yes	No
1. frequent buyer programmes?	____	____
2. frequent referral programmes?	____	____
3. thank-you cards?	____	____
4. newsletters/personal letters?	____	____
5. telephone recalls?	____	____
6. customer reward and recognition programmes?	____	____
7. customer special events?	____	____
8. strategic alliances or partnerships?	____	____

These eight ideas are all customer retention policies which are also good marketing strategies for your business. The more 'No' answers you have, the more programmes you will have to develop and implement to retain your customers.

1. Frequent buyer programmes

Frequent buyer programmes are similar to the airlines' frequent flyer programmes. You are rewarding those customers who buy from you regularly. The rewards do not have to be expensive or lavish; they just have to show the customers that you appreciate their business. Be sure that it is easy for all your regular customers to benefit from this programme.

Consider a retail store that punches a card every time you buy something. After your tenth or twelfth purchase, you get something free or at a significant discount. This policy encourages you to go back to shop there because you will receive a special reward when you meet a specific criterion. Repeat purchase cards are an excellent way to retain customers, and they are also an excellent marketing tool.

2. Frequent referral programmes

If your business depends on referrals, you should reward the people making referrals to you. Your rewards will also reinforce their behaviour, thereby creating a positive cycle and a mutually beneficial relationship.

The best way to use a frequent referral reward programme is to develop it in tiers or levels. Here are some suggestions for rewards based on the number of referrals from one source. Don't forget to fill in how you would reinforce this behaviour. Also, feel free to change the reward recommendation to suit your business or situation.

Number of referrals	Reward recommendation	My reward
1	Thank-you card	
2	Telephone call	
3	Flowers	
4	Small gift (under £5)	
5	Gift certificate (dinner for two)	

When the same person refers more than five people, do something special for that person. Then start the referral reward programme all over again.

If your customers don't mind having their names visible in your shop or office, create a referral thank-you bulletin board.

Put the names of your current customers who refer new customers to you on this board each month. You can also indicate the number of referrals they have made. People usually like to see their name written on something, and this will give them the satisfaction of knowing that you appreciate their efforts. Also, it may create healthy competition among your customers to see who can refer more new people to you each month. They benefit because you will reward and reinforce them and you benefit from the new business and positive word of mouth.

Create a new customer welcome bulletin board. List the names of your new customers each month. This is the first step in a proactive customer retention programme. When people see that you care enough to put their name up for everyone else to see, they will go out of their way to help you in your business and to remain loyal to you.

3. Thank-you cards

A simple and effective customer retention technique that few businesses exploit, writing a thank-you card and sending it to someone who has bought something from you, takes only a little extra effort. Cards are the best postage-stamp marketing investment you can make.

If you do not want to write out a card for every customer who buys, have your cards preprinted with a message that shows your appreciation. It is even more effective if you develop part of your customer retention programme around a series of these cards.

Here are samples of preprinted cards that I use for all my customers. You can have them done at your local printer or buy them from a special dealer. The cards are sent out in the order you see them: 'Thank you for your business'; 'Our customers are number 1'; and when the job is completed, 'It was a pleasure to work with you'. When my company receives a referral, we send out the referral thank-you card. All this information and the dates on which the cards are sent are recorded on our customer database.

Front

THANK YOU
for your Business

Inside

𝒲e value your business highly
and hope to be of service to you
many times in the future.

Company name here

Front

**OUR CUSTOMERS ARE
NUMBER ONE WITH US!**

Inside

**WE APPRECIATE
YOUR BUSINESS AND
THANK YOU FOR THE
OPPORTUNITY
OF SERVING YOU!
YOU CAN ALWAYS COUNT
ON OUR SUPPORT!**

Company Name Here

Front

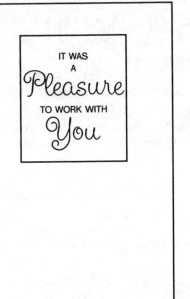

IT WAS
A
Pleasure
TO WORK WITH
You

Inside

*H*ope we get the
opportunity to do it again
in the near future.

Company name here

Front

Thank You
for your
Referral

Inside

*Y*our confidence in us is
greatly appreciated.

Company name here

4. Newsletters/Personal letters

Newsletters are a great way to keep your customers informed
of what is going on in your business. You can tell them whatever information you need them to know. And, because it is
coming from you free of charge, they will be only too glad to
read it.

One way to keep your customers involved with your business is to promote contests or other activities in the newsletter. Specify that they come to your shop or office to win the contest. This is another good time to solidify their loyalty and make sure that you retain them as customers.

One variation of the newsletter is a letter of news. Write a personal letter to each customer (a computerised customer database makes this task very easy) and mention all the items that you would have mentioned in a newsletter. Your customer will be pleased that you took the time to write them a personal letter. Here is an example of a one- to two-page letter of news:

Sample – personal letter

Today's date

Michael Mitchell
Any House
Anytown

Dear Michael Mitchell

I just wanted to thank you for continuing to do business with us. I also wanted to take this opportunity to tell you about some of the great things that are happening in our business and how they can benefit you. As you know, we have provided both marketing, consulting and training services for you in the past year. Your comments indicated that you were very satisfied and are interested in working with us again. Here is some exciting news to help you decide when we can begin these programmes.

New Marketing Book Is Published

I have recently had a marketing book published in the United States. It is called *Writing and Implementing a Marketing Plan* and is available to all our marketing consulting clients free of charge. I am hoping that it will be published in the UK soon.

Corporate Videos Being Filmed

Several large corporations have asked us to film their presentations to prospective clients. Our videos are professionally produced using state-of-the-art equipment. They can be as long as you need to get your message across. We provide all the necessary services, including script writing, filming, editing, sound, pre- and post-production.

The Last Training Seminar You Will Ever Need

It has taken more than 20 years of research in psychology, human behaviour, human relations and communication. Now we have designed a training programme that can help you to achieve greater personal and professional success, more sales, more friendships, deeper and more meaningful relationships and a better love life. It is called *Success Through Effective Human Relations*, and it teaches you about people's behavioural and interpersonal styles, sensory perceptual communication styles and the basic principles of effective human relations. The programme is customised to suit your needs and budget.

I hope this information has been helpful to you. Please feel free to phone me if you have any questions. Or just drop in to see us and say hello. We appreciate you as our customer, and we look forward to continuing our relationship with you.

Yours sincerely,

Richard F Gerson, PhD

PS Look out for my latest book, *Keeping Customers for Life*, which will soon be published by Kogan Page. It will provide you with many ideas on how to get and keep customers for life.

5. Telephone recalls

Telephone recalls work well in any type of business. If you are in a service business where customers need to make appointments, you can phone them a day in advance to remind them of the appointment. Or, if they have not been in to see you for some time, you can phone them to see how they are doing and to inform them of a reason to come in now to do business with you.

If your business is retail, you can phone customers personally and invite them to a special sale. Department stores often send mail shots to their credit card holders inviting them to a sale before the general public is invited. If this makes you feel special, think how much more special you will feel when someone phones you personally.

When you are not able to make all the calls personally, write out a basic script for the caller. You want your message of caring for the customer to come across loud and clear.

When your customers phone you, treat them with courtesy. Answer the phone in the following way: 'Good (morning, afternoon), (company name), this is (your name). How may I help you?'

Never put a caller on hold for more than 30 seconds without coming back and telling them what the delay is. People hate waiting, and they will hang up and take their business elsewhere. If your customers complain that they cannot get through to you on the telephone, it may be time to install more telephone lines.

Some businesses use the telephone as their life's blood. Do not make the mistake of neglecting the telephone as a way of retaining your customers. Phone them regularly, even if it is just to say hello.

6. Customer reward and recognition programmes
Recognising and rewarding your customers should be a regular business practice. Sending thank-you cards tells customers that you recognise their importance to your business. Giving them gifts for referrals shows them how much you appreciate their efforts on your behalf. Offering them rewards for making repeat purchases tells them that you understand their contribution to your business success. But you can do more to retain customers.

First, recognise every customer who does business with you.

Learn and use their names. If you cannot remember someone's name, at least acknowledge that you recognise that person as a regular customer. If someone is a new customer, go out of your way to learn his or her name and everything you can about him or her. Your interest will be appreciated.

Next, make your customers feel important. Many businesses say that they do this, but it is just not so. You have to give extra effort to make customers feel important, and once you do, you will keep them for life.

In what ways can you make them feel important? Try these suggestions:

- Ask them about their family, especially their children or grandchildren.
- Congratulate them on some achievement or a job promotion.
- Ask for their advice on something related to your business.
- Tell them they look nice.
- Give them a surprise just for doing business with you.

You can probably think of several more ways to make people feel important. They key is to do this in a natural manner so that each individual customer feels and believes that you are taking a special, sincere interest in him or her.

You can recognise and reward your customers in other ways. Invite your customers to special sales or give them special treatment. Hold a contest for your best customers and give the winner a trip as a grand prize. Give other winners gift certificates or dinners at restaurants. Print VIP cards for your best customers that entitle them to extra discounts.

All these ideas are strictly customer retention ideas – they have nothing to do with serving the customer during the time of a purchase. Yet they are vitally important to the success of your business because they create added value for the customer.

It is easy for a competitor to price merchandise the same as you do, to give the same type of guarantees as you, and to provide the same extensive and courteous service as you. If that happens, the only thing that will make a customer choose to do business with you is the value-added service that you provide.

The chart below will help you to create your own customer recognition and reward programme. Use the first column to describe the customer's action, the second to show that you recognise that behaviour of the customer, the third to explain how you will reward that behaviour. Remember, it is better to create a shorter list and do those things extremely well than to try to do a lot of things adequately.

Customer action	How recognised	How rewarded
Samples		
First referral	Thank-you note	Small discount
Second referral	Telephone call	Box of chocolates
High volume purchase	Telephone call	Meal
_____	_____	_____
_____	_____	_____
_____	_____	_____

Employee recognition and reward programmes
Any customer retention programme must include recognition and rewards for your employees. Remember that they are your customers too, and on some occasions they are your most important customers. Show them that you care about them as much as you do about the external customers. Create a recognition and reward programme for your employees just as you did for your customers in the last section.

When you treat employees as customers, their morale will improve, and they will want to do well for the company. Furthermore, they will want to continue working for you. Customers like to see the same faces all the time. Both your customers and your employees will enjoy the stability. People like doing business with people they know and like. Long-term employees provide that for you with your customers. Therefore, never

forget or neglect your employees. Always treat them as customers. It is as important to retain them as it is to retain your
external customers.

7. Customer special events

Special events for your special customers are a great way to
strengthen the relationship. Many companies have special
sales for the general public while others have private sales for
their credit card holders. You too can create a special event for
your best customers.

Host a cocktail party or other social gathering at your place
of business after hours. Invite several good customers to dinner
at a nice restaurant. Treat them to a round of golf, tickets to a
sporting event or show, or do something special for their
families.

Special events for special people do not have to be elaborate
or expensive. They only have to be special. Ask your customers
what is important and special to them. Then wait a short while
and give them what they want and like. They will reward you
with their loyalty.

8. Strategic alliances or partnerships

You would keep more of your customers if you made more of
them your partners. This is not as crazy an idea as it may seem
at first. You do not have to make your customers financial partners in your business. Rather, you make them partners in
doing business. Here are a few suggestions.

Site visits

Invite your customers to spend a day with you at your place of
business. Let them go anywhere they please, ask questions of
anyone, and even try to work for a while. Ask them to view
everything with a critical eye.

Having them on site can be of tremendous benefit to you.
First, it shows them that you care enough to invite them into
your business. Second, it tells them that you think they are
important, because you are asking their opinion on how to
improve your business. Third, it helps you to get an objective

opinion from an outsider on how well your business is running.

After you invite customers on site, the next step in creating the strategic partnership is for you to visit your customers. This may be at their place of business, at their homes (depending on how friendly you have become with them) or at a social function. If you want to make customers strategic partners, you must become intimately involved with them. You must also offer to help them, just as they are helping you.

This idea of strategic partners may not be as new to you as you may think. Don't you work with one accountant? Do you have a personal physician? How many financial planners or stockbrokers are you working with? How many suppliers are you working with? How long have you been working with these people?

All these relationships are strategic partnerships. You are helping these people to succeed just as they are helping you to succeed. Why shouldn't you do the same thing with your customers? Remember that it is easier and less expensive to do business with an existing customer than to acquire a new one. And you will have more existing customers if you create more strategic partnerships.

Customer as sales agent
Customers who perceive themselves as strategic partners for your business become your best sales agents. They will tell others what a pleasure it is to do business with you. These new customers will come to you with a positive attitude because you have already been endorsed by someone they trust. It is up to you not to let the new customers down.

On the other hand, customers who are not your strategic partners may not say anything good about you. They may not say anything bad, but they also may not say anything at all. No reference means no sale for you.

Therefore, try to make every customer a strategic partner. They can help you more than you know. And, even if there is someone who does not become your customer today, plant the seed for a strategic partnership in the future. You will be glad you did.

Retention through recovery

Not all customers are happy customers. Sometimes you have to make up for bad service or a bad product. Service recovery means actions that tell the customer you will take care of his or her problem. Restitution is what you give your customers to compensate them for their inconvenience. You should welcome any situation that requires service recovery and restitution.

Most recovery and restitution opportunities result from customer complaints. These complaints do not have to be loud or demanding. They can be very quiet and, sometimes, almost go unnoticed. Yet, if you reread the 'Startling service statistics' (page 17) concerning the number of people who don't complain compared to those who do, you will find that you should welcome complaints as a part of doing business. If someone complains, they are taking the time to help you improve your business. You, then, must take the time to acknowledge and resolve their complaints.

Every business or organisation will have to face the fact that some time, some customer will be unhappy, dissatisfied or upset with their product or service. It is your responsibility to resolve the problem as quickly as possible to the customer's satisfaction.

You probably already have some type of recovery and restitution programme in place. Use the chart overleaf to outline your programme. Fill in the spaces in each column. Then read on to see if your programme does all it could do.

Satisfying unhappy customers

Customers who complain feel annoyed, cheated or victimised. They also feel that their situation is the most important in the world. Understand these feelings and treat your customers accordingly. Dissatisfied customers tell up to 20 friends that they are unhappy with the way you do business. However, if you resolve their problems, 50–74 per cent of these same customers will do business with you again. Adapt the following five-step recovery programme to your business and specific

Policy	Procedure	Exceptions (?)	Recovery/ Restitution
Returns	30 days w/receipt	(Fill in here)	Exchange product

situation, and then train your employees to be sure that it is implemented.

Service recovery programme

1. *Apologise*
   First and foremost, say that you are sorry for the incon-venience caused to the customer. Be sincere – the customer will notice if you are not. A sincere apology usually defuses the customer's anger. Also, you must personally accept responsibility for the problem occurring and its resolution.

2. *Urgent restatement*
   Restate the problem as the customer described it to you to make certain that you understand exactly what the cus-tomer means. Then tell (and show, if possible) the customer that you will do everything possible to solve the problem and resolve the complaint immediately. Even if you can't resolve the problem to his fullest satisfaction, the customer

will perceive that you were sincere and definitely intended to help. His dissatisfaction will diminish.

3. *Empathy*
   Make certain that you communicate clearly with your customers so they understand that you know how they feel. Do not patronise or try to pacify them. Just show them and tell them you understand how they feel. Use phrases such as: 'I understand . . .', 'I know how you feel . . .', 'I can see why you're upset'.

4. *Restitution*
   Here is your chance to score points. Not only will you take immediate action to resolve your customers' complaints, such as refunding their money, making an exchange or offering a credit, you will go a step further. Tell and show your customers that you will make it up to them in some special way. You may have to provide them with a free gift for their trouble or you may have to allow them to buy a new item at a sale price. Whatever you do, look at it as adding value rather than spending extra money.

5. *Follow-up*
   This is where most programmes fail. Be sure to find out if your customer is satisfied. You can ask a simple question or two at the end of the recovery process: 'Have we resolved your complaint to your satisfaction? What else may we do for you?' Then wait a few days and phone the customer to make certain that he or she is still satisfied. You can also send a letter. A nice touch would be to enclose a coupon or gift voucher with the letter. Going the extra mile will help you to create and keep a loyal customer. Also, keep track of what you did and said as well as how the customer responded. This will help you the next time the customer does business with you.

Use this basic five-step approach to service recovery and restitution as a guide to develop a workable programme for your business. You may want to break the restitution down into resolution (the action taken to resolve the complaint) and restitution (anything else that you do for the customer to compensate for their inconvenience). Whatever you do, this programme will also help you to consider service recovery and restitution as part of a larger complaint management programme.

Managing complaints for customer retention

This basic approach to handling a complaint and keeping a customer is also a unique sales opportunity. A customer is more motivated to buy from you at the time you have taken special care of him or her (resolved the complaint) than at any other time. Once you have resolved the complaint to his or her satisfaction, you can begin working on a new sale. Use the 10 suggestions on turning customer complaints into additional sales to create loyal and long-term customers for your business.

Turn customer complaints into sales

1. Understand why the customer is complaining. Most probably, a need has not been satisfied or an expectation has not been met.
2. Listen attentively. The customer wants your undivided attention and respect concerning this problem, and he or she deserves to get it.
3. Handle one complaint at a time, even if the customer has several. You can manage a single complaint most effectively and have a better chance of turning that complaint into a sale than trying to handle two or three complaints at once.
4. Ask the customer what the needs were at the time of purchase and why those needs are not now being met. Find out how the current needs differ from the original, and why the change occurred.
5. Tell the customer that you understand the complaint and that you are sorry there is a problem. Assure the customer that you will do everything possible to resolve the complaint immediately.

6. Once you have resolved the complaint, discuss new sales offers and their benefits.

7. Handle any objections you may receive to the new sales offer, and continue to manage the original complaint if it comes up again.

8. Attempt to close the new sale resulting from the customer complaint as if it were an original sale. Sometimes, these 'complaint sales' are easier because the customer has already made a purchase and knows how your product or service can satisfy a need.

9. If you cannot resolve the complaint to the customer's satisfaction, offer alternatives such as speaking to a person of higher authority, exchanging the merchandise or refunding his or her money.

10. More than 75 per cent of the people who complain and have that complaint resolved immediately will make another purchase. Use this statistic to your advantage as you continue to try to close the sale to the 'complaining' customer.

How to CARE for your customers

When resolving a service or performance problem, you must show the customers that you CARE about them. If you CARE, your customers will reward you with their loyalty. To CARE properly for your customers, you must be:

Credible. Credibility, or your reputation, is really all you have in the business world. Customers must believe in your product or service, your customer service policies and procedures, your performance efforts and those of your staff. If they don't believe in you, they will not buy from you. Customers buy only for four reasons: to save or make money, to save time, to feel secure (have peace of mind) or to boost their egos. If you promise that your product or service will do one or more of these four things for your customers, it had better perform. If it doesn't, you must implement your service recovery programme to ensure their satisfaction and loyalty are maintained.

Accessible. Customers want to be able to access your customer service system quickly and easily. They are already upset about something. Don't make it more difficult for them by passing them from employee to employee. Be accessible and customer friendly.

Reliable. Customers want to know what to expect from your business. You must do what you say you will do at the time you say you will do it. You must get it right the first time, get it done for the customer on time, and then check with the customer to ensure satisfaction. Reliability comes from the consistency in the performance of your product or service and the consistency with which you treat customers. When you are reliable, customers know what to expect from you and they feel comfortable doing business with you.

Excellent. You and your employees must strive for excellence all the time. Don't accept anything less. Customers believe that they themselves are important and excellent, and they want to do business with excellent companies and people. Provide excellent customer service and you will have excellent customer retention. Provide excellent training programmes for your staff and you will have excellent performers who will ensure retention of your customers. If your work isn't excellent, it isn't good enough. Your customers want excellence and so should you.

Retaining your customers must become part of your regular business life. Follow the five basic steps for recovery and restitution, manage complaints so that you can turn them into additional sales, and CARE for the customer. If you do so, you will keep your customers for a long time.

Retention through training

Untrained employees present a bad image of your company. If your workers understand your product or service but cannot speak and listen to customers, you will not be in business very long. If your customers don't get the attention they deserve, they will take their business elsewhere.

Employee training is frequently an underused and under-developed method of customer retention. Most companies train their employees how to do their jobs but not how to interact with customers. Both are equally important.

Recent statistics estimate that if a company spends 2–5 per cent of its annual payroll on employee training, it should realise about a 10 per cent increase in net profit. Furthermore, companies with superior customer service and a loyal customer base can charge up to 10 per cent more than their competitors. So if you train your employees to provide superior customer service, your net profit can increase by 20 per cent.

Types of training programmes
You can provide many types of training programmes for your employees. The most important programmes for customer retention are:

- Customer service: company policies, systems and procedures
- Team building: developing cohesive and self-directed teams
- Communication skills (includes effective listening)
- Sales training basics (everybody sells).

These four programmes are not difficult to implement. If your company does not have the resources to develop them, outside consultants can provide training in these areas. To find these consultants, contact the Institute of Training and Development (ITD)* or your local college of higher education. These organisations will be able to direct you to qualified trainers who can help you to develop and implement employee training programmes in conjunction with your customer service and retention programme.

If you decide to work with an outside consultant or trainer to upgrade the skills of your employees, you will probably go

*Contact the ITD at Marlow House, Institute Road, Marlow, Buckinghamshire SL7 1LB; tel 0628 890123; fax 0628 890208.

through the same process that others do when they decide to do business with you. People choose to do business with someone for reasons such as convenience, price, location or personal referral. Remember that when people choose you, they are your customers, and when you choose a trainer for your company, you are that trainer's customer.

The evaluation criteria questionnaire that follows represents the processes that people go through when selecting a consultant or a business provider. Answer these questions accurately. They will help you to select the person or training firm you need.

Evaluation criteria questionnaire

1. Does the consultant (business) demonstrate complete understanding of my problem, situation or needs?
2. Has the consultant (business) fully and accurately explained the approach (product or service) that will solve my problem?
3. Do I think the proposed approach will be successful?
4. What resources are available to make me a satisfied customer?
5. Is the consultant (business) qualified to provide me with the products and services I need?
6. Is the behavioural, communication and service style of the consultant (business) compatible with my own?
7. Will my problem be solved, or will my needs be met quickly?
8. Is the consultant (business) experienced enough for my situation?
9. Is the cost of the product or service fair, and am I getting good value for my money?
10. Do the references of the consultant (business) confirm the level and quality of service that I will be receiving?

Use these questions as a guide when selecting a trainer to develop the skills of your employees. Choose your consultant carefully. Remember – when you train your employees, they will perceive that you truly care about them. Not only will they provide superior service to your customers, they will also provide you with superior performance, productivity and loyalty. When you train your staff well, you, your business, your employees, your customers – everyone – wins.

Retention through rapport and effective communication

Every time you interact with a customer it is a moment of truth. It is a chance for you or your employees to represent the company positively and satisfy a customer. These interactions will succeed or fail depending on how well rapport is established and how effectively you communicate with the customer. The skills for building rapport and strengthening communication are easily learned.

When a customer comes to you to make or exchange a purchase, request information or register a complaint, that customer wants to be heard. You must be an active and attentive listener so that you can understand how the customer perceives the current situation, even though you may perceive it differently.

You and your customer each interpret any given situation based on your behavioural style and sensory perceptions. We are all a combination of four behavioural styles: dominant, expressive, solid or analytical. Certain characteristics make up each type, which are shown in the personality factors chart on page 52.

You must know how to respond to your customers based on their particular behavioural styles. For example, a dominant customer is impatient and wants to control the situation to ensure that he or she gets the desired results. Analytical types will be very precise and compliant with your rules for customer service and can be extremely persistent with their questioning. The 'Service situation planner' on page 53 will help you to respond to each behavioural type.

If you can respond appropriately to each behavioural type, you will develop rapport with that person. You can increase this rapport by 'pacing' your customer. Pacing means that you mirror their body language, rate of speech, vocal tones and even eye movements.

Try to use the same words, phrases, slogans and slang that your customers use, because their words will tell you their sensory perceptual style: visual, auditory or kinaesthetic. A visual person speaks in pictures, images and sights. An auditory person talks about sounds, hearing and harmony. A kinaesthetic person describes a situation in terms of feelings, senses and touch.

Behavioural styles: Personality factors

DOMINANT
- Goal oriented/results oriented
- Impatient
- Task oriented/high achiever
- Workaholic
- Decisive
- Opinionated/stubborn/blunt
- Innovative
- Tough/firm in relationships
- Control oriented
- Competitive/loves challenges

EXPRESSIVE
- Dreamer
- Unrealistic goals
- Creative; ideas flow
- Needs approval and compliments
- Generalises
- Persuasive, outgoing
- Opinionated
- Fast decisions
- Excitable
- Enthusiastic, shows confidence

SOLID
- Needs people
- Good listener
- Status quo/dislikes change
- No risks
- No pressure
- Counsellor/helps others
- Questioning
- Insecure/needs reassurance
- Supportive
- No conflict

ANALYTICAL
- Planner/organiser
- Details/technicalities
- Slow decisions
- Must be right
- Conservative/cautious
- Low pressure
- Precise/critical/logical
- Problem solver
- Persistent
- Follows procedures/compliant

Behavioural styles: Service situation planner

Dominant

- Goal oriented/results oriented
- Impatient
- Task oriented/high achiever
- Workaholic
- Decisive
- Opinionated/stubborn/blunt
- Innovative
- Tough/firm in relationships
- Control oriented
- Competitive/loves challenges

'D' Dominant
Be clear, specific, brief and efficient.
Stick to business.
Present the facts logically.
Ask specific (preferably 'what') questions.
Provide service choices.
Provide facts and figures about the results of your service.
If you disagree, take issue with facts, not the person.
Motivate and persuade by referring to objectives and results.
Support, maintain, use discretion.

Expressive
- Dreamer
- Unrealistic goals
- Creative; ideas flow
- Needs approval and compliments
- Generalises
- Persuasive, outgoing
- Opinionated
- Fast decisions
- Excitable
- Enthusiastic, shows confidence

'E' Expressive

Plan interaction that supports their feelings/intuitions. Be stimulating. Use enough time to be sociable, yet fast-moving.

Leave time for relating, socialising after completing service encounter.

Talk about people, their goals, opinions they find stimulating.

Don't discuss extensive details related to service.

Ask for their opinions/ideas regarding how to service them better.

Provide ideas for implementing action.

Provide testimonials from people they perceive as important, prominent.

Offer special, immediate and extra incentives for their willingness to accept your service offer.

Continue supporting the relationship, be casual.

Recognise their accomplishments.

Solid
- Needs people
- Good listener
- Status quo/dislikes change
- No risks
- No pressure
- Counsellor/helps others
- Questioning
- Insecure/needs reassurance
- Supportive
- No conflict

'S' Solid

Start (briefly) with a personal commitment. Be agreeable.

Show sincere interest in them as people.

Listen well. Be responsive and supportive.

Elicit personal goals and work to help achieve these goals as related to service.

Ask 'how' questions.

If you agree easily, look for possible areas of their dis-agreement or dissatisfaction.

If you disagree, look for hurt feelings.

Be informal, orderly and friendly.

Guarantee their decision will minimise risks.

Offer clear, specific solutions with guarantees.

Analytical
- Planner/organiser
- Details/technicalities
- Slow decisions
- Must be right
- Conservative/cautious
- Low pressure
- Precise/critical/logical
- Problem solver
- Persistent
- Follows procedures/compliant

'A' Analytical

Approach them in a straightforward, direct but low-key way; stick to business.

Support their logical, methodical approach; build your credibility by listing pros and cons of your service approach.

Present specifics and do what you say you can do. Take your time, but be persistent.

Create a schedule to implement service actions with step-by-step timetable. Assure them there won't be surprises.

If you agree, follow through and document for the record.

If you disagree, make an organised presentation of your position and ask for their suggestions to resolve the situation.

Give them time to verify predictability of your actions; be accurate, realistic.

Provide solid, tangible, practical evidence and options for future service performance.

Provide long-term guarantees.

Rapport and effective communication are enhanced when you use the same type of words that your customer uses. If your customer says, 'It sounds to me like this product is not working properly,' do not respond, 'I see what you are saying.' You should answer, 'I hear what you are saying. What sound tells you that the product is not working properly?'

When you establish good rapport and communication with your customers, they will want to continue doing business with you and will refer others to you. The result is more business and more customers staying with you for a longer period.

When your customers say that they enjoy doing business with you because you are so much like them, you understand them, you know almost exactly what they are thinking and you provide excellent service, you have received one of the greatest compliments any businessperson can.

Sensory perceptual style processor equivalents
Every sensory perceptual style has its own language by which it processes information. The language of one style has an equivalent in the other two styles. These are called processor equivalents. It is up to you, and necessary for your complete understanding of sensory perceptual styles, to identify these and other terms related to each particular style. For example, anything to do with seeing or images is visual, hearing or sounds or speaking is auditory, and feeling or touch is kinaesthetic. The list overleaf provides you with some of these processor equivalents.

Once you identify that the words someone uses belong to a specific sensory perceptual style, you must match those words and style to achieve rapport. This may mean that you have to change your sensory perceptual communication style for a particular situation because you want to communicate successfully.

Visual	Auditory	Kinaesthetic
See	Hear	Feel
Look	Listen	Touch
Bright	Loud	Pressing
Picture	Sound	Feeling
Colourful	Melodious	Exciting
Illuminate	Be heard	Be felt
Clear	Harmonious	Fits
Dawn	Tune in	Firm
Flash	Crescendo	Spike
Appear	Discuss	Aware
Perspective	Expression	Hands-on
Focused	Listen to	Secure
Foggy	Off-key	Clumsy
Strobe	Harsh	Irritate
Form	Resonance	Angle
Visual	Vocal	Do/act
Imagine	Speak	Be
Perception	Attention	Action
Blank out	Inner voices	Fidget

CHAPTER 3
50 Ways to Keep Your Customers for Life

You're almost there. So far, we've talked about customer service and going beyond customer service. Now here's a list of 50 things you can do to secure, satisfy and retain your customers for life.

1. Create a service-oriented culture
Everyone in the company must be customer service oriented. All employees must realise that they work for the customer, and their job is to ensure the ultimate satisfaction of the customer. Everything else is superfluous.

2. Have a service vision
A vision is vital to the service success of any organisation. A vision is more than just a philosophy of doing business. The vision must be the corporate cultural ethic. Everyone must believe and live the vision for your company to provide excellent customer service and keep customers for life. Management may develop the vision, but the staff must make it a reality.

3. Total support
True success comes from total organisational support. It may be top management who decides to embark on a customer service programme, but it is the line employees who implement the programme. If these people don't support the initiative, the programme won't work. Total support is needed.

4. Policies in writing

To benefit both your customers and your employees, put your service policies in writing. This way, there can be no mistakes or misunderstandings. Be aware, however, that your employees should have the authority to grant discretionary exceptions to the policies when the need arises. Remember – policies are guidelines, and they must remain flexible.

5. Employee empowerment

Give your employees the authority to go with their responsibility of satisfying and keeping the customer. Allow them to make decisions on the spot and support those decisions. Remember that their job is to satisfy the customers and keep them coming back. Employees should not have to look for you or a manager every time a customer needs something out of the ordinary.

6. Employee training

Train, train and then retrain to retain your employees. Give them on-the-job training, off-the-job training, tapes, books, seminars, workshops – anything that will help them to do their jobs better. While you may find qualified people who have just left school, nothing prepares a person better for handling customers than the training that they receive on the job and in practically applied programmes.

7. Marketing the service programme

All your marketing should communicate that you provide superior customer service, are interested only in total customer satisfaction, and will do everything possible to keep your customers. This message must be stated in everything that you send out to the public and the trades.

8. Recruit good people

Take on people who are good and well qualified. Innate people skills go a long way towards helping your staff to provide superior customer service and retain your customers.

9. Don't make customers pay for service

Pay for anything related to customer service, including delivery charges on returns, long distance telephone calls, postage and anything else the customer is normally charged. If you don't pay for the cost of service, your competition will, and then your customers will become their customers.

10. Reward loyalty

What gets rewarded gets done. If you reward both customers and employees for their loyalty, they will both stay with you a long time. The rewards must be perceived as valuable by the recipient, but they do not have to cost you much money.

11. Inspect what you expect

What gets measured gets done. Measure the performance of your staff and you will see an increase in performance levels, quality and productivity. You will also ultimately see an increase in profitability.

12. Set standards of performance

Let everyone know exactly what they must do to provide superior customer service. Make these standards as objective and measurable as possible, even though you may provide an intangible service. When people achieve these performance levels, customer retention and loyalty naturally follow.

13. Trade jobs

Get your employees to work in other departments. They will develop an appreciation of what other people in the company do, and therefore no employee will blame another for a customer problem. In fact, since the employees have experience in other areas, they will be able to solve more problems and satisfy more customers on the spot.

14. Cross train

Train your employees in other people's jobs. They will be able to provide more assistance to customers, more assistance to each other, and you will become less dependent on 'irreplace-able' employees when they are not at work.

15. Easily accessible service systems

Make your customer service systems easy for the customers to access. Make sure that they are put through quickly to some-one who can help them when they phone up; ensure that they speak to an employee who can help them as soon as they arrive at your place of business. Don't make it hard for customers to come to you. They may decide not to do business with you again.

16. User friendly service systems

Make your customer service systems easy to use. The cus-tomer is the reason for your business, not someone who is in the way of doing business. Make the customers feel and know that they can bring a problem to your attention, voice a com-plaint, get it resolved as quickly as possible and receive superb treatment during all their contacts with your company.

17. Design flexibility into your service policies

Keep your policies flexible, because each customer and situation is different. Your employees must know that they can modify a written or stated policy to ensure the customer's total satisfaction at any given moment, and you *must* support your employees' decisions and actions in these situations.

18. Educate the customer

Do not assume that the customer knows what you know. Use every customer contact as a chance to educate the customer about something related to your business. Even if you are just educating them about your great returns policy, teach them. They will be appreciative and show this by continuing to do business with you.

19. Handle complaints properly

Acknowledge that the customer is upset, listen carefully, assure him or her that you are doing everything possible at this moment to resolve the complaint, and then resolve the complaint. Then, when he or she expresses appreciation for your efforts, use the opportunity to increase loyalty. Thank the customer for bringing the problem to your attention, apologise again for the problem and try to sell the customer something else.

20. Turn complaints into additional sales
The customer is most receptive to continuing to do business with you after you resolve a complaint. Using this opportunity to make a sale is both ethical and practical. Your customers will appreciate your interest in them. They will probably buy from you now and go out and tell their friends how well and quickly you handled their problem. You will develop a reputation for credibility, reliability and honesty.

21. Train your employees to do it right the first time
Repair, rework and additional free services are very costly. Doing it right the first time guarantees greater profitability, happier customers and more long-term customers. If you must do something over again for a customer, do it even better the second time.

22. Every customer has a lifetime value
When a customer buys from you, that purchase is not a one-off, one-price deal. Consider the potential that customer brings to your business. How much money could that customer spend with you over a lifetime? That amount is the lifetime value of a customer and that is the type and level of service he or she should receive every time business is done with you.

23. Beg for customer feedback
It is not enough to send out surveys or leave comment cards at the cash register. You must get as much customer feedback as possible, even if you have to beg for it. If customers are asked for their opinion and see that you have implemented their suggestions, they will not only continue to do business with you, they will recommend that friends come to you too. Do what-

ever you can to solicit their opinions and comments, and then act on their suggestions.

24. Identify customer values, beliefs and standards

Your service programmes must be geared to the values, beliefs and standards of your customers. If customer values and your values conflict, invite your customers into the business for a discussion to find out why the difference exists and what can be done about it. Then decide if you must modify your position to maintain customer satisfaction and loyalty. However, you should never compromise your ethics and values to satisfy a customer.

25. Get and use employee ideas

Your employees who have daily contact with customers know more about what customers need, want and expect than you or any other manager could ever hope to know. Get feedback from your employees, listen carefully to their suggestions and implement as many as possible. Research shows that the best service companies not only get more ideas from their employees, they use more of them. This makes employees feel wanted and cared about and shows them that you think as much of your internal customers as you do of your external customers.

26. Be fair and consistent

Customers may not always like or agree with what you do for them, but as long as you treat each one fairly and consistently, they will respect you for it. Consistency enhances your credibility and reliability which are essential for building loyalty and retaining customers.

27. Underpromise and overdeliver

Customers' expectations can be unrealistically raised when businesses overpromise and underdeliver. Usually the business cannot meet these expectations, and the customer goes away disappointed. But if you set realistic expectations for the customer on your quality and level of service and then exceed those expectations, the customer is more than satisfied.

Remember, though, that you should not underpromise to the extent that you insult your customers. They will see through you in a minute and take their business elsewhere.

28. Compete on benefits, not products or prices
Customers can always find another product at a lower price, somehow, somewhere. You must always remind your customers of the benefits of doing business with you. Features can be found in every product, but benefits are unique to the way in which you do business.

29. High touch is more important than high tech
High tech does get people to say 'wow!', but it doesn't get people to care about other people. Your business needs high touch to survive. Stay close to your customers. Get to know them well. The closer you are to your customers, the longer they will do business with you. After all, when you show you care, you become like one of the family.

30. Ask customers what they want
Constantly ask your customers what they want from you, what you can do for them and how you can do it better. They may want a new product or service, extended hours or just something minor that will make them happier. You will never know unless you ask. After you ask, you must give them what they want. They will reward your generosity with loyalty.

31. Daily service management
Every employee in every department is involved in providing superior service to achieve the ultimate goal – keeping the customer for life. Do everything possible to make everyone's job easier so that it will be easier for them to give the customers what they want. If there is a problem during the day, make the necessary adjustments and resolve it quickly.

32. Know the cost of losing a customer
All employees should know the lifetime value of a customer, the cost of losing even one, and the effect that loss can have on

your business. Consider rewarding your employees if they retain your customers over a longer-than-average period.

33. Know your competition
What kinds of customer service are your competitors providing? What are they doing to retain their customers? Are they offering more benefits, better service policies, or are they just being nicer to the customers? Find out, and if they are doing something you are not doing, then do it. If it works for them, it will probably work for you.

34. Conduct market research
You can never have enough information about your customers. Do surveys, interviews, whatever it takes to find out what the marketplace wants. Then adapt your business accordingly. Information is not power unless you know how to use it.

35. Conduct internal assessments
Constantly evaluate your company's customer service, satisfaction and retention. Interview your employees, have them fill in questionnaires, ask your customers at the point of purchase how you are doing, and then use this information to improve your service and retention efforts. Examples of simple surveys for you to use are provided in Appendix 2.

36. Know what your customers need, want and expect
Businesses run into problems when they think customers need, want or expect one thing when they really require another. These gaps in perception about service delivery ultimately disappoint customers. Find out what the customers need, want and expect, and then give it to them.

37. Find, nurture and display customer champions
Every business has one, two or several employees who are true customer champions. Find out who these people are, nurture and support them, then make them role models for everyone else to follow. Reward their behaviour. The rest of your staff will upgrade their service performance to this level to receive

similar rewards. The result is a highly motivated, service-oriented staff, and a group of satisfied and loyal customers.

38. Effective communication is critical to success
Every problem between people is the result of poor communication. Train your people to develop effective communication skills: how to listen first, how to speak so others will listen, how to understand others before trying to be understood, how to receive and give feedback, and how to develop rapport with customers.

39. Rapport is the key to successful communication
The technical skills of communication can be acquired and used, but without rapport there is no communication. The skills of developing rapport can be taught and your employees should learn them. When employees and customers have rapport, there is a feeling of trust and a desire to continue to do business.

40. Smile
Smiling is important when serving a customer. Smiles will usually get a smile in return, but smiles will not guarantee quality customer service. Smiling must be something that employees do because it makes them feel good, and it makes the customers feel good.

41. Make customers feel important
The more important you make customers feel, the better they will feel about doing business with you. Call them by name, ask them to tell you about themselves and ask questions about their accomplishments. Your reward will be a lifetime customer.

42. Promote your customers
With their permission, of course, use your customers in your marketing and promotion efforts. Let them tell their story to other customers and prospects. This third party endorsement fosters tremendous credibility, and your customers will love being involved.

43. Create a customer council
Your customer council, like a board of directors, should meet regularly to scrutinise your business and the service you provide. The council makes suggestions on which you act.

44. Market frequent buyer programmes
To get your customers excited about doing business with you, start a reward programme for frequent buyers. You can use coupons, punch cards or anything else that helps you to keep track of customer activity. When purchases reach a certain level, reward your customers with a gift – a high discount coupon, a free product or service or something more expensive, such as a trip.

45. Accept only excellence
If you expect average performance and service, that is what you will get. So set your expectations high. Accept only excellent performance from your employees, and train your staff to achieve these levels of performance. Good enough should never be good enough.

46. Employees are customers too
Employees are your internal customers, your first line of customers, and each of them has a customer somewhere in the value chain. Each employee must provide excellent customer service to every other employee so that they can all provide superior service to customers. This is the only way to guarantee customer satisfaction and retention.

47. Let customers know you care
Send them thank-you cards, postcards and anything else you can to show them you care. Never let them forget your name. Teach them that whenever they need something, they can come to you for it because you care. Spend time and money marketing your caring attitude to your customers.

48. Make service results visible

Visibility enhances credibility, and credibility is only enhanced by improved performance. Put your customer comment cards and letters where all your customers see them. Create a testimonial book for customers to read. Put employees' performance results on the noticeboard in their staffroom or cloakroom. Make service results visible so that your employees will constantly improve and your customers will be the beneficiaries of this improved service.

49. Go the extra mile

When customers want something from you, give it to them. Then do something extra. They will be grateful and you will have a long-term customer.

50. Marketing and customer service go hand in hand

All your marketing efforts should communicate your customer service message. In today's competitive marketplace, the only thing that differentiates companies is the level and quality of their customer service, and this is the major criterion that people use to decide whether or not to continue purchasing from that company. Customer service is a very effective and powerful marketing tool, and marketing is a very effective and powerful customer service tool. Combined, the two will help you to keep your customers for life.

Now review everything you are doing and make it better

Whatever you are doing now to service and satisfy your customers may not be sufficient to keep them tomorrow. A competitor will offer superior customer service on a better product at a lower price that has more benefits. You have to stay one step ahead of your competitors. You must know what they're doing and how they're doing it. Review your customer service policy, then do whatever it takes to make it better

Remember – you are in business to make money, and the only way you will make money is to have satisfied customers who keep coming back.

APPENDIX 1

Customer Service Tips and Lists

10 Commandments of superior customer service and retention

1. The customer is the most important person in the company.
2. The customer is not dependent on you – you are dependent on the customer. You work for the customer.
3. The customer is not an interruption of your work. The customer is the purpose of your work.
4. The customer does you a favour by visiting or phoning your business. You are not doing customers a favour by serving them.
5. The customer is as much a part of your business as anything else, including stock, employees and your facility. If you sold the business, the customers would go with it.
6. The customer is not a cold statistic. The customer is a person with feelings and emotions, just like you. Treat the customer better than you would want to be treated.
7. The customer is not someone to argue with or match wits with.
8. It is your job to satisfy the needs, wants and expectations of your customers and, whenever possible, resolve their fears and complaints.
9. The customer deserves the most attentive, courteous and professional treatment you can provide.
10. The customer is the lifeblood of your business. Always remember that without customers, you would not have a business. You work for the customer.

Tips for long-term customer retention

- Call each customer by name.
- Listen to what each customer has to say.
- Be concerned about each customer as an individual.
- Be courteous to each customer.
- Be responsive to the individual needs of each customer.
- Know your customers' personal buying histories and motivations.
- Take sufficient time with each customer.
- Involve customers in your business. Ask for their advice and suggestions.
- Make customers feel important. Pay them compliments.
- Listen first in order to understand the customer. Then speak so he or she can understand you.

Customer's bill of rights

The customer has a right to the following:

1. Professional, courteous and prompt service.
2. Your full and undivided attention each time the customer chooses to do business with you.
3. Quality products and services.
4. Fulfilment of needs in a manner consistent with reasonable service expectations.
5. Competent, knowledgeable and well-trained staff.
6. Attention to every detail every time they access your customer service system.
7. The benefits of all your resources, teamwork and networks to provide superior, long-term service.
8. Open channels of communication for feedback, complaints or compliments.
9. A fair price for your products or services.
10. Appreciation from you and your staff for past and future business.

7 Checkpoints to successful customer retention

1. Have a clear customer service mission, vision and philosophy. Communicate this to your employees, then train and empower them to carry out your service mission.
2. Provide customers with quality products, services and care.
3. Listen closely to your customers, and then act on their suggestions. Do the same for your employees.
4. Pay attention to your own intuition when serving customers, and have your employees pay attention to theirs.
5. Treat customers with respect, trust, fairness, honesty and integrity.
6. Communicate with your customers regularly, including existing customers, former customers and your competitors' customers.
7. Expand your product and service offerings carefully, ensuring that you can continue to provide quality customer service while you grow.

10 Greatest customer service and retention tips of all time

1. Unique service philosophy
Businesses need a unique service philosophy or mission statement, which should complement their overall business mission statements. The service philosophy should describe exactly how customers will be treated when they purchase products and services from you and your preferred outcomes for every service encounter.

2. Customer feedback
Get customer feedback in any way you can. Set up customer councils, hand out surveys in your place of business, mail out surveys, conduct personal interviews, and beg your customers for feedback. The more you involve customers with your business, the more they will tell you how to improve it. Listen, evaluate the information, and act on the suggestions.

3. Service and retention programmes
Use your customer service system and your customer retention programme as powerful marketing tools. Phone your customers, send them thank-you cards and postcards, mail them newsletters. Do anything and everything you can to keep them informed about your business. The more they see your name, the greater the probability that they will continue to do business with you.

4. Close the gap
What customers expect from a business can be quite different from what they receive. The same holds true for what the business thinks customers want and what the customers actually want. Work to close these gaps so your perceptions of situations coincide with those of your customers.

5. Meet and exceed expectations
Customers have expectations which they bring to every business situation. You must meet these expectations to satisfy the customer. You must exceed these expectations to ensure their long-term loyalty. Exceeding expectations is the key to retention and repurchase.

6. Customer reward programmes
What gets rewarded gets done. Any type of reward programme aimed at the customer, such as frequent buyer or referral programmes, will motivate the customer to continue purchasing from you. Rewards make the customer feel special, and customers will return to the source of that special feeling. Do this for your employees too.

7. Public identity
The identity you create for your business must match the identity customers perceive of themselves. Identity is just one factor customers use in deciding to purchase from you. The image and identity you create in the community, backed up by your actions, influences when and for how long customers buy from you.

8. Community service

Community service, charity tie-ins and environmental issues have a large influence on customer expectations. Make sure that your customers know of your efforts in these areas. Your community service will help them to feel good about doing business with you.

9. Easily accessible, user-friendly service systems

Make it extremely easy for customers to get service from you. When they need something, have it for them, including new products, returns, refunds, solutions to complaints or anything else they need. Keep your rules, regulations, policies and procedures flexible. They should be guidelines, not laws.

10. Train and empower your employees

Quality employees provide quality service. Train your employees to do their jobs and provide superior customer service. Then give your employees the authority to make decisions to satisfy the customer, even if it goes against company policy. Support your employees in all their decisions to satisfy and keep the customer, because without customers there is no business.

One last thought!

Always remember that your employees are your first line of customers. These internal customers must be treated with the same care, respect and importance as your external (buying) customers. If you want your employees to provide superior service and work to keep the customers, you must provide superior service to your employees and work to keep them.

APPENDIX 2

Customer Service, Satisfaction and Retention Surveys

The importance of self-assessment and evaluation cannot be overemphasised. The following series of surveys will help you to evaluate your customer service efforts, including how well you provide service, how well your staff provide service, and how satisfied your customers are with your service. The results of these surveys will indicate your customer service strengths and weaknesses. In all surveys, the higher the number the more favourable the response. Feel free to adapt the surveys to suit your particular needs.

Customer service self-assessment

Respond to each statement by placing the number that best describes your answer in the space provided. Use the following scale:

1	2	3	4	5
Never	Rarely	Sometimes	Usually	Often

1. I accept people without judging them. _____
2. I show patience, courtesy and respect to people regardless of their behaviour towards me. _____
3. I maintain my composure and refuse to become irritated or frustrated when coping with an angry or irate person. _____
4. I treat people as I would want them to treat me. _____

1	2	3	4	5
Never	*Rarely*	*Sometimes*	*Usually*	*Often*

5. I help others to maintain their self-esteem, even when the situation requires negative or critical feedback. _____

6. I do not become defensive when interacting with another person, even if their comments are directed at me. _____

7. I realise that my attitude towards myself and others affects the way I respond in any given situation. _____

8. I realise that each person believes his or her problem is the most important and urgent thing in the world at this time, and I try to help them resolve it immediately. _____

9. I treat everyone in a positive manner, regardless of how they look, dress or speak. _____

10. I view every interaction with another person as a 'golden moment', and I do everything in my power to make it a satisfactory and win-win situation for both of us. _____

Service rating scale

Using a scale of 1 to 10 with 10 being the best, please rate how well you and your staff provide each of the following services:

Service	Self	Staff
a. Prompt and courteous answering of the telephones	_____	_____
b. Accurate responses to telephone enquiries	_____	_____
c. Providing individual and personal attention to each client	_____	_____
d. Marketing and promoting the business to current and new clients	_____	_____

e. Marketing and promoting the business to
    professional and other referral sources   _____   _____

f. Communicating prices and invoicing
    procedures clearly and concisely   _____   _____

g. Providing high quality, courteous and
    friendly service to all clients   _____   _____

h. Requesting and quickly resolving customer
    complaints   _____   _____

i. Keeping clients informed and updated
    about current and new developments
    regarding the business   _____   _____

j. Tracking the effectiveness of marketing
    and service efforts   _____   _____

Customer service survey

We are interested in finding out what you think about our
services. Please respond to each statement by placing the number of the appropriate response in the blank space next to the
statement.

1	2	3	4	5
Never	Once in a while	Half the time	Often	Very often

1. The telephone is answered by the third ring.   _____

2. The person answering the telephone is courteous
    and friendly.   _____

3. I am placed on hold for more than 30 seconds.   _____

4. My call is directed to the appropriate person.   _____

5. The office (shop) is conveniently located and
    easy to find.   _____

6. There is ample parking available near the office
    (shop).   _____

7. The atmosphere of the office (shop) is warm and
    inviting.   _____

1	2	3	4	5
Never	Once in a while	Half the time	Often	Very often

8. The regularly scheduled office (shop) hours are convenient for me. _____

9. The salesperson or the service provider greets me immediately. _____

10. I wait less than 15 minutes if my appointment is delayed. _____

11. Prices are appropriate for the products and services provided. _____

12. Payment terms for the products or services are flexible. _____

13. Payment methods are acceptable. _____

14. I receive good value for my money. _____

15. The office (shop) staff are courteous and friendly. _____

16. The service provider and/or staff are courteous and friendly. _____

17. I receive personalised attention and service. _____

18. My complaints are resolved quickly and to my satisfaction. _____

19. The service provider and/or staff answer all my questions to my satisfaction. _____

20. The service provider and/or staff are concerned about my situation. _____

21. I am involved in decisions regarding my purchase. _____

22. I feel comfortable with the personality of the service provider (staff). _____

23. I am kept informed of all details regarding my purchase. _____

24. I am happy with the way the service provider (staff) treats me. _____

25. I feel the service provider (staff) is qualified to provide me with these services. _____

26. I prefer to use these services rather than those provided by someone else. _____

1	2	3	4	5
Never	*Once in a while*	*Half the time*	*Often*	*Very often*

27. I can make an appointment or shop at the store when it is convenient for me. _____
28. I will use this service provider (store) again. _____
29. I would refer people to this service provider (store). _____
30. The overall quality of the service is high. _____

Thank you for completing this survey. Your answers will help us to understand your needs and improve the quality of the services we offer to you.

Customer satisfaction questionnaire

We are interested in finding out how satisfied you are with the services and treatment you received. Please respond to each question by placing the number of the appropriate response in the blank space next to the statement.

1	2	3	4	5
Extremely dissatisfied	*Slightly dissatisfied*	*Neither satisfied nor dissatisfied*	*Slightly satisfied*	*Extremely satisfied*

How satisfied are you with:

1. The location of the office (shop)? _____
2. The parking around the office (shop)? _____
3. The office (shop) opening hours? _____
4. The office (shop) atmosphere and decor? _____
5. The telephone manners of the staff? _____
6. The treatment you receive from the staff? _____
7. The treatment you receive from the service provider? _____

1	2	3	4	5
Extremely dissatisfied	Slightly dissatisfied	Neither satisfied nor dissatisfied	Slightly satisfied	Extremely satisfied

8. The prices for the services? _____
9. The payment methods and terms? _____
10. The quality of the services? _____
11. The qualifications of the service provider? _____
12. The manner in which your complaints are handled? _____
13. The manner in which your questions are answered? _____
14. The professionalism of the staff? _____
15. The marketing and advertising programmes of the service provider? _____

APPENDIX 3
Customer Information and Profile

The best way to satisfy and retain your customers is to know as much about them as possible. You should know their likes and dislikes, their buying histories, their needs and wants, and anything else that will help you to seem more personable to them. Your goal is always to maintain their loyalty and retain them as customers.

Most companies are now computerised, either at the point of purchase or behind the scenes. If you have a customer database, use it. It is your most effective service and marketing tool. If you do not have a computer for your business, the two forms overleaf will help you.

Your customers may complete the classification information form or it can be filled in by your staff, who ask the customers the questions. The customer profile should be filled in by your staff so that all the necessary information is captured on the form. As always, you are free to adapt the forms to suit your business and specific situation.

Keeping Customers for Life

Classification information

To learn more about you and to continue providing you with high quality service, we would appreciate it if you would fill in the requested information. Thank you.

Name: _____

Address: _____

Town: _____ County: _____ Postcode: _____

Telephone: (H) _____ (B) _____

Age: _____ Gender: M _____ F _____

Marital status:

Married ____ Single ____ Divorced ____ Widowed____

Family size: _____ Occupation: _____

Education completed:

School _____ University _____

College _____Vocational/Trade _____

Date of last visit: _____

Household income: (Tick one)

£10,000 – £19,999 _____

£20,000 – £29,999 _____

£30,000 – £39,999 _____

£40,000 – £49,999 _____

£60,000 – £69,999 _____

£70,000 +   _____

Customer profile

Name: _____ Telephone: _____

Address: _____

Town: _____ County: _____ Postcode: _____

Personal information:

Date of birth: _____

Spouse's name: _____ Children: _____

Characteristics/Likes/Dislikes: _____

_____

Special interests/Hobbies: _____

Business information:

Company name: _____ Title: _____

Telephone: _____

Secretary's name: _____

Reports to: _____ Title: _____Ext: _____

Office contacts: _____

Purchasing authority: _____Volume: _____

Purchase habits/Preferences: _____

Currently buys from: _____

Satisfaction level: _____

Needs/Benefits/Solutions:

Current needs: _____

Future needs: _____

Current problems: _____

Benefits/Solutions: _____

Call date: _____ Response: _____

Next call: _____ Action: _____

Further Reading from Kogan Page

Customer Care, Sarah Cook, 1992
Customer Service, Malcolm Peel, 1988
Know Your Customers! Jay Curry, 1992
Managing Quality Customer Service, William B Martin, 1991
Measuring Customer Satisfaction, Richard F Gerson, 1994